MEASURING UP
size

Peter Patilla

Thameside Press

Distributed in the United States by
Smart Apple Media
1980 Lookout Drive
North Mankato, MN 56003

Text copyright © Peter Patilla 1999

Illustrator: Dave Cockcroft
Editor: Claire Edwards
Designer: Simeen Karim
Picture researcher: Juliet Duff
Consultant: Martin Hollins

Library of Congress Cataloging-in-Publication Data

Patilla, Peter.
    Size / written by Peter Patilla.
        p. cm. -- (Measuring up)
    Includes index.
    Summary: Examines the ways in which capacity has been measured and discusses how
    area, volume, and other units of measure have evolved.
    ISBN 1-930643-16-0
    1. Mensuration--Juvenile literature. [1. Measurement.] I. Title.

QA465 .P345 2001
530.8--dc21   2001023425

Printed in USA

9 8 7 6 5 4 3 2 1

Picture acknowledgments:
Ancient Art and Architecture: 6, 7 Brian Wilson; 10 left; 21. **Bridgeman Art Library:** 12 and
22 V & A Museum. **Camera Press Ltd:** 4 Mike Davis. **Werner Forman Archive:** 8. Robert
Harding Picture Library: 5 Picture Book Ltd; 7 top left Dominic Harcourt-Webster. **Michael
Holford:** 9. **Science Photo Library:** 13, 23 Jean-Loup Charmet; 14 Rosenfeld Images Ltd; 25;
front cover, 28 Tom Van Sant/Geosphere Project, Santa Monica. **Science and Society Picture
Library:** front cover b, 10 right; 16. **Tony Stone Images:** 15 James Jackson; 17 Dennis O'Clair;
18 Joseph Sohm; 20 Ken Whitmore.

CONTENTS

WHAT'S IN A SIZE?

We use all sorts of sizes in our everyday life. Many words describe size. Large things are huge, gigantic, massive, and jumbo. Small things are minute, minuscule, micro, and mini. But these words don't always help. A jumbo chocolate bar is small compared to a minivan.

Size may refer to length, weight, capacity, volume, or area. Sometimes you need to know what kind of size you are referring to, and to be able to measure it accurately. This can help you make useful comparisons. This book looks at measures of capacity, volume, and area, and at how they have developed.

Shoe sizes

Shoe sizes are based on length, but they are given special shoe size numbers. English shoe sizes were first used in about 1305. At this time King Edward I stated that 1 inch should measure three barleycorns in length, and a child's shoe that measured 13 barleycorns became size 13. Nowadays, children's shoe sizes in England begin at size 0 and go up to size 13. The sizes of shoes still increase in intervals equal to one barleycorn. In America, children's shoe sizes start at 2 for infants and go to 12 for toddlers.

Did you know?
In the Middle Ages, pointed shoes were very fashionable. Some shoes had points that were 17³/4 inches (45 centimeters) long. King Edward III of England banned shoe points longer than 2 inches (5 centimeters).

Confusing shoes

Buying shoes in different parts of the world can be very confusing. American shoe sizes are different from British ones. A size 5½ in the U.S. is only a size 4 in Britain. Metric shoe sizes in the rest of Europe are worked out by measuring a foot in centimeters and dividing this length by two thirds. To complicate matters, men's and women's shoe sizes differ from each other.

Some people like very large T-shirts, some like them just right. Runners and cyclists need to wear tight, streamlined clothes.

Clothing sizes

Another type of size you come across every day is clothing sizes. These are sometimes based on the length and width of material and marked S, M, L, and XL. These letters stand for small, medium, large, and extra large.

Cooking sizes

The size of a measure is very important in cooking. Some people cook by taking a pinch of this and a pinch of that, but recipes require more accurate measurements. Some measures are given as weights; others as cups or spoon sizes. There are several different sizes of tablespoon. In the U.S. a tablespoon holds a little under 0.5 oz (14.2 ml). In Britain it can hold 0.5 or 0.6 oz (15 or 17.7 ml) and in Australia it holds 0.8 oz (20 ml). A teaspoon in each country holds 0.16 oz (5 ml). These are level, not rounded, measures. Cooks usually measure small amounts of liquid using milliliters, fluid ounces, or fractions of a cup, marked on the side of a jug.

MEASURING CAPACITY

Capacity is a measure of how much something will hold. Over the years, it has been measured with many types of units.

There is a close link between capacity, volume, and weight. Thousands of years ago, people needed to weigh things out and compare weights. But they soon realized that, although things such as single objects were easy to weigh, other goods were easier to measure by capacity.

Dry measures

Goods such as grain and spices (which are often called dry goods), as well as large quantities of bigger items, were often measured in scoops or containers, where they couldn't slide off or spill out. Sometimes a scoop was used to measure amounts that were too small to be weighed accurately.

Liquid measures

Because liquid doesn't have a shape of its own, weighing liquids is not very practical. People found it much easier to measure wine, oil, and vinegar in different kinds of containers, such as gourds or jugs. The amount they held sometimes became a measure of capacity.

Gourds are a hard-shelled fruit. They have been used as containers for thousands of years, and are still used today in some countries.

First measures

The first measures of capacity, or how much something would hold, were natural objects, such as eggshells, seashells, or the hard shells of fruits. These were also used as scoops to fill larger containers or to measure out certain amounts. The size of a container was measured by counting how many scoops were needed to fill it. The problem with using natural objects as a measure is that their size varies. So people began to invent standard measures that everyone could use.

Standard measures

Probably the first people to use standard measures of capacity were the Babylonians in about 2150 B.C. They measured liquid in a hollow cube. Each side of the cube measured the width of one hand, or about 4 inches (100 millimeters). This unit of capacity was called a *ka*. The weight of water that the *ka* held had to be equal to the Babylonian weight called a great *mina*, which was just under 2 lbs (1 kilogram). There were also larger units of capacity called *gin* and *gur*. A *gur* was 300 *ka*, or 60 *gin*, and was equal to about 79.25 gallons (300 liters).

Did you know?
In the past, people used containers whose names became units of capacity. The Germans used a *canne* and a *glas*. The Italians used a *botta* and a *pinta*.

These ancient spoons were used in the first century to measure medicines.

EARLY UNITS OF CAPACITY

As countries began to trade with each other, units of capacity became more standard, especially those used to measure grain and wine.

One of the most important measures used by the Ancient Egyptians was a cubit—the distance from the elbow to the outstretched fingertip (about 20 inches or 50 centimeters). To measure capacity, the Egyptians made a cube where each side measured a cubit. This cubic cubit held about 147 quarts (140 liters) and was used to measure goods such as grain and wine. The Egyptians also used other standard units of capacity called, from large to small, *ro*, *hin*, *hekat*, and *khar*.

Ancient Greeks

The Ancient Greeks were traders in the Mediterranean region from about 1000 B.C. They traded large amounts of oil and wine. Like the Babylonians and Egyptians, the ancient Greeks based their liquid capacity measure on a unit of length. They called it a *metretes*, and it held about 10.3 gallons.

This wall painting was found in an Egyptian tomb. It was painted in about 1400 B.C. and shows government officials measuring grain after the harvest.

These large jars were used by the Romans to measure and store oil and wine.

Did you know?
Medieval market-places had fixed stone containers. Traders had to use these as standard measures for their corn.

Roman measures

When the Romans conquered Greek lands in about the second century B.C., they became the most powerful nation in the world. Their main unit of capacity was a *sextarius*, which was about 1¼ pint. They used the *sextarius* and the *amphora* to measure dry and liquid amounts. The Romans also used units called *hemina* and *modius* to measure dry amounts, and *quartarius* and *urna* to measure liquids.

After the Romans

When the Romans left their conquered lands in Europe, Asia, and Africa, people continued to use Roman measures. These were adapted by local people and by other conquerors such as the Vikings and Arabs. Like measurements of length and weight, the units of capacity varied from area to area, and even between neighboring towns. This made trade rather difficult.

Laying down the law

In Britain, different kings tried to make people agree to use the same units of measurement, but with little success. In 1215, King John signed an important document called the Magna Carta, which set a standard for many English laws and rules. One of the things he ordered was that there must be "one weight and one measure" for all the people. It gave the units for dry amounts. For example, corn was to be measured by the cartful and was to be called the London quarter.

BUSHELS

By medieval times, a bushel was used in Europe to measure dry goods such as grain, fruit, and vegetables.

The first record of a standard bushel was the Winchester standard, in A.D. 850. It was a unit of capacity that held about 2,150 cubic inches. It was divided into smaller units called pecks, gallons, quarts, and pints. There were two pints to a quart, four quarts to a gallon, two gallons to a peck, and four pecks to a bushel.

This scene shows corn measurers in Paris striking a measure of grain.

Striking a bushel

In 1296, King Edward I of England passed a law that said the measure called a London quarter should be exactly eight striked bushels. The word *striked* was important. When people were measuring, they would talk about a measure being heaped, striked, or hollow. When the measuring container was piled high over the top, it was heaped. When it was not quite full, it was hollow. When a stick was drawn over the top to level the contents, it was struck. A striked measure means level to the brim.

This standard Winchester bushel was made in 1601, during the reign of Queen Elizabeth 1.

10

British and American bushels

When English settlers went to America, they took their measures to their new home. In the early 1800s, the British government passed laws that introduced imperial measures. These changed the size of existing measures, such as the bushel. But the laws did not affect American colonies, so an American bushel became smaller than the English one.

Cheating with bushels

Because settlers came to America from many different parts of Europe, standard bushels varied from state to state, which caused much confusion. From the mid-nineteenth century, the Office of Weights and Measures provided standard measures for each state to enforce. In 1901, the U.S. government set up the National Bureau of Standards, which today is called the National Institute of Standards and Technology. This continues to set the standards. The bushel is no longer a legal measurement in the U.S.—cubic yards or cubic feet are used instead.

Size Fact
A bushel of apples weighs less than a bushel of potatoes. The unit remains the same, but potatoes have more mass.

Pecks

A peck was a quarter of a bushel. Its name came from an old Greek word, *bikos*, meaning wine jar or beaker. It also became a specially sized pot for measuring grain, and became a fixed unit of capacity.

GALLONS AND PINTS

Gallons and pints are standard units of liquid capacity. They were once also used to measure dry goods, but a pint of beer was not the same as a pint of corn.

Did you know?
The capacity of a full stomach is about six cups of liquid.

No one knows exactly when the gallon was first used. After 1600, it became a standard unit for measuring liquids in Britain, but it had been used for a long time before that.

A choice of gallons

At first there were three standard gallons, each one a different size. From largest to smallest, there were standard gallons for measuring ale, grain, and wine. In 1707, Queen Anne of England passed a law that changed a gallon of wine to a new standard size.

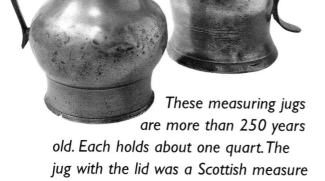

These measuring jugs are more than 250 years old. Each holds about one quart. The jug with the lid was a Scottish measure called a tappit hen.

Two gallons too many

In 1824, the government decided that three standard gallons were two standards too many. They set a standard for a new imperial gallon. This was any container that held 10 pounds of water (4.536 kilograms). Americans continued to use the earlier Queen Anne gallon, which had been introduced by settlers. So American gallons are smaller by a fifth than those used in Britain.

This picture shows the reception room of an important French pharmacist (apothecary) in the eighteenth century. People are mixing and measuring medicines as accurately as possible.

Quarts, pints, and gills

A gallon is divided into smaller units called quarts, pints, and gills. There are four gills to a pint, two pints to a quart, and four quarts to a gallon, which makes eight pints to a gallon. The imperial pint was the standard measure of liquid capacity in Britain until the metric measuring system replaced it with the liter. The quart and pint are still used in the U.S.

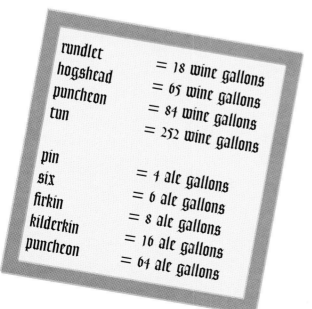

rundlet	= 18 wine gallons
hogshead	= 65 wine gallons
puncheon	= 84 wine gallons
tun	= 252 wine gallons
pin	
six	= 4 ale gallons
firkin	= 6 ale gallons
kilderkin	= 8 ale gallons
puncheon	= 16 ale gallons
	= 64 ale gallons

Measuring medicines

In the past, pharmacists were called apothecaries. They developed their own units for measuring liquid called minims, drams (also spelled *drachm*), and fluid ounces. A dram was also the name of a unit of weight. A minim was about one drop of liquid. There were 60 minims in one dram, eight drams in one fluid ounce, 20 fluid ounces in an imperial pint, and 16 fluid ounces in an American pint.

Other units of liquid capacity

In the past, gallons, quarts, and pints were the standard units used for measuring liquid capacity, but there were other units as well. Many were used to measure wine and ale. They had wonderful names such as hogshead and puncheon, and were mostly named after different types of containers. The name of the container told someone what size it was because, like the gallon, each had been standardized in well-known units.

MORE CONTAINERS

Today, we still describe a measure of liquid using the name of its container, such as a bottle of coke, a glass of milk, or a barrel of oil.

Small amounts of oil are stored in barrels, also called oil drums. There are 42 U.S. gallons or 35 imperial gallons in a barrel of oil. Oil is produced at a rate of about 22 billion barrels each year.

Before there were shops and supermarkets, people had to store all they needed in their homes. They stored goods such as grain and fruit in large sacks, barrels, and crates.

Did you know?
There is enough water in the human body to fill about one and a half large buckets.

Barrels
Barrels have been used for hundreds of years to store and measure liquids and dry goods. They have different capacities, depending on what they are used for. In the past, craftsmen called coopers made barrels to store soap, butter, and ale. From about 1530, each cooper had to have his own sign stamped on his barrels. If the size was wrong or the wood not good enough, the cooper was fined. Half the fine went to the king, and half went to the person who reported him. By law, only coopers could make soap and ale barrels.

Big bottles

A standard wine bottle has a capacity of 26 fluid ounces or 75 centiliters. But there are much bigger bottles than this. A magnum holds two bottles. A jeroboam holds four bottles. A methuselah holds eight bottles, a balthazar holds 16 bottles and a Nebuchadnezzar holds 20 bottles.

Glasses

Glasses come in all shapes and sizes. Their shape can easily fool people into thinking they hold more than they really do. Some glasses, called schooners, have narrow middles. This means they hold much less than if they were straight all the way down. Ice cream glasses are usually wide at the top but narrow at the bottom. This makes them easy to eat from, but they do not hold as much as they seem to. A sphere-shaped container holds the most liquid for its size.

These glasses are sundae glasses. They do not hold as much as they seem to, because of the narrow bottom and thick glass.

Butts

Butts were special large barrels used for storing liquids. They usually held about 525 quarts. The word *bottle* comes from butt. The person who looked after the butts and bottles in a house was called the butler. Today, water butts are often used to store rain water.

Bottles and cartons

Nowadays, we buy all sorts of liquids in bottles, and their sizes vary. Luckily, a bottle of medicine is likely to be smaller than a bottle of coke. Although there is no single standard bottle size, one of the most common sizes holds about 33.8 fluid ounces or one liter. Many liquids come in cartons, too, and cartons often hold 64 fluid ounces or one-half gallon.

LITERS AND MILLILITERS

The main units of capacity in the metric system of measuring are liters and milliliters. Liters are used to measure large amounts of liquid; milliliters are used to measure small amounts.

The first person to develop the idea of a metric system was a French priest named Gabriel Mouton. In 1670, he outlined the three most important things about a metric system. These were to: a) use 10 as the basic unit; b) to use standard prefixes such as deci, centi, and milli; and c) to use measurements of the Earth as a basis for working out the standard metric units.

Equality for all

It was not until the French Revolution, which began in 1789, that Mouton's idea of a metric system was developed and adopted. Many of the thinkers and leaders of the French Revolution wanted to make life fairer and more equal for everyone. They wanted to make a new start without kings and queens and the old systems of government. They thought that one way to do this would be to develop a fairer system of measurement. Before the Revolution, people used so many different measures and they varied so much, that it was hard to make sure traders always treated people fairly.

These metric measuring cylinders range from 1 centiliter to a liter.

Metric around the world

Napoleon Bonaparte was a brilliant soldier who became ruler of France after the Revolution. Gradually, as his armies conquered most of Europe, they tried to make other countries follow French law and use French weights and measures. Slowly the metric system began to be used almost everywhere. Officially, Britain adopted metric measures in 1963, but they were not widely used until the 1970s. Gallons and pints are still used alongside liters and milliliters. The U.S. is the only large country to use the old measures. In 1866, the metric system was made legal, but not obligatory, in the U.S.

Pipettes are used to measure small amounts of liquid accurately. They are measured in milliliters or cubic centimeters.

The metric system

French scientists settled on three standard measures for length, weight, and capacity. These measures relate cleverly to each other. A meter (length) is one ten-millionth of a line drawn from the North Pole to the equator, passing through Paris. The kilogram (weight) is one thousandth of the weight of water in a meter cube. The liter (capacity) is one thousandth of the amount of water needed to fill a meter cube. A liter of water weighs one kilogram. A milliliter of water weighs one gram, and one milliliter of water has a volume of a one centimeter cube.

Did you know?
There are about 5 quarts of blood in the human body.

UNUSUAL CAPACITY

Standard units of capacity are usually used to measure dry or liquid goods. But there are some unusual and unexpected everyday capacities, too.

This baseball stadium has a large capacity so that many people can watch the match. Stadiums are named after an ancient Greek length known as a stadion. The Romans adopted this length and called it a stadium.

The size of buildings and vehicles is sometimes given in relation to how many people they can hold. An audience can be described as a capacity audience, which means that all the seats are full. Theaters and buses have a seating capacity, which gives an idea of how large they are. Large theaters may have a capacity of thousands.

Amphitheaters

Amphitheaters are round or oval buildings with seats all around a central stage. One of the largest and most famous amphitheaters is the Colosseum in Rome. It was built in about A.D. 70, and had a seating capacity of 50,000 people. The word *colossal* is still used today to describe anything that is huge.

Safe seating

A car also has a seating capacity that can vary from a two-seater sports car to a stretch limo seating 12 or more people. Although a car has a safe seating capacity, people often try to fit more in. As many as 102 people have tried to climb into a Volkswagen Beetle at one time.

Car engines

Inside a car's engine, there are cylinders and pistons that power the car. The capacity of the cylinders is measured in liters and tells you the size of the engine. A 2-liter car has cylinders that hold 2 liters of fuel vapor and gases. The Bugatti Royale, built in 1927, had eight cylinders inside its engine, with a huge capacity of 12.7 liters.

Computer capacity

Computers and computer disks store information in an electronic memory. The data is stored in the form of binary numbers, each one called a bit. Eight bits make a byte, and about a million bytes make a megabyte. The size of a computer's memory is a type of capacity and is measured in megabytes. The storage capacity of a floppy disk is about two megabytes.

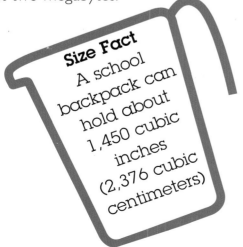

Size Fact
A school backpack can hold about 1,450 cubic inches (2,376 cubic centimeters)

Air capacity

Our lungs have a capacity for air, which is measured in liters. Full lungs hold about 3 liters of air. A normal breath takes in about 0.5 liters, but a sprinting athlete breathes about 70 liters of air a minute.

Did you know?
In one day an adult breathes enough air to fill 1,000 party balloons.

VOLUMES AND PI

Volume and capacity are very closely linked. Capacity is how much something holds, while volume is how much space something takes up. We refer to a barrel's capacity, but the grain inside it has volume.

If you have a hollow cube with very thick walls, its volume will be greater than its capacity. The cube will take up more space than it will hold. Volume is measured in cubic units, such as cubic feet, or cubic meters.

Did you know?
The word *volume* comes from a Latin word *volumen*, which means something rolled up, such as a scroll. Scrolls were replaced by books, which are still called volumes today.

Timber is still sold in units of volume rather than by weight. It is stacked in piles like the original cords of logs.

Building materials
Some building materials are bought by units of volume. Rough-cut timber is measured in units of volume called cords. A cord was originally a pile of 8-foot long logs, measuring four feet high by four feet wide, tied with a cord. Sand, gravel, and cement can be bought by volume (cubic yards) or weight (tons).

Early mathematicians
Finding volumes has practical uses, and the methods to do it have been worked out by the most brilliant mathematicians in history. Since ancient Egyptian and Babylonian times, people have found clever ways of calculating volumes of shapes, such as cubes, pyramids, cylinders, and spheres.

Curved volumes

Archimedes is also famous for working out a number that allowed people to calculate areas and volumes of objects that had curves in them. This special number is called *pi*. Pi is the Greek letter for *p* and is written π.

Pi (π)

π is calculated by dividing the circumference of a circle by its diameter. The answer is always the same. It comes to a number slightly more than 3. Mathematicians all around the world have been trying to calculate the exact value of π for hundreds of years. Early this century, a brilliant Indian mathematician named Srinivasa Ramanujan developed ways of calculating π that were so clever they are used by today's computers. Mathematicians often use 3.142 as the value for π, but computers have worked it out to more than 100,000,000 decimal places. The digits that make up π never make a repeating pattern.

Archimedes was a brilliant Greek engineer and mathematician. He designed war machines to defend his home town in Sicily, and was killed by a Roman soldier in about 212 B.C. when the Romans attacked the town.

Bath mathematics

Archimedes, a famous Greek mathematician, was born in Sicily in about 287 B.C. There is a story that one day as Archimedes climbed into his bath, he noticed how the water level rose. This gave him the idea for working out the volume of irregular shapes. When something is put under water, it pushes water out of the way to make room for itself. The volume of water that rises equals the volume of the object put in the water.

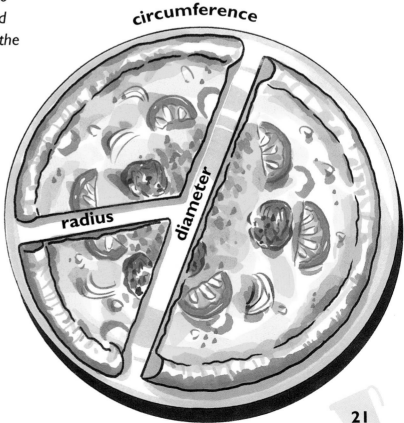

AREA AND PERIMETER

Area is a kind of size that tells you how much surface something covers. All through history, area has been an important measure.

Calculating area has been important for all sorts of people, including engineers, farmers, artists, tailors, and builders. If you are buying a piece of land or a piece of fabric, it is no use knowing just the length or just the width. But by knowing the length and the width, you can work out the size in a useful way. Area is measured in square units, such as square feet or square meters.

The first measures of area
The earliest standard unit of area appeared in Ancient Egyptian and Babylonian times, based on the area of a field. During plowing, a plow made furrows about 23½ inches (60 centimeters) wide. The number of furrows in a field helped people to calculate its size.

A Roman *actus*
In Roman times, land was measured in a long thin unit called an *actus*, which was 120 Roman feet long by two furrows wide (about 120 feet by 4 feet or 36 meters by 1.2 meters). These thin strips were arranged in horizontal or vertical groups. When 30 strips were arranged side by side they made a square *actus*, which was a good size for a small family farm.

All through the ages, farmers have plowed long straight furrows the same distance apart. These helped them to measure their land.

Acres of land
In Britain, during the sixth century, areas of land began to be measured in acres. The word *acre* probably comes from the Latin word *ager*, which means field. An acre was the area a team of oxen could plow in a day. Later, an acre became an area of any shape of land that measured 43,560 square feet (4,047 square meters).

Modern measures

Acres are still used today as a measure of the size of land, especially in the U.S. In many countries, land is measured in metric units called hectares. A hectare is 10,000 square meters, or about 2.5 acres.

These chocolate configurations have the same area, but different perimeters.

This page is from a book by Euclid called **Elements.** *It was written in about 300 B.C.*

Did you know?
In about 300 B.C. the Ancient Greeks measured the perimeter of their coastline using knotted ropes thrown over the sides of their ships.

Brilliant Greeks

Calculating the area for more difficult shapes has fascinated mathematicians for thousands of years. Two of the most brilliant mathematicians were Greek. They were Pythagoras, who lived in the sixth century B.C., and Euclid, who lived in the third century B.C.. Their work on shapes and areas is still used today. Euclid wrote one of the most important math books ever, called *Elements*. Part of it describes how to calculate areas of different shapes.

Perimeter

Shapes that have the same area can look very different. Even though their area is the same, the distance all around them may be different. The distance all around a shape is called its perimeter. An accurate measure of a piece of land gives its perimeter as well as its area. In medieval Europe, plots of land were often described by giving areas in acres and perimeters in rods. A rod was 16.5 feet (5 meters) long.

MEASURING AREAS

Measuring the area of a square or rectangle is quite simple. All you have to do is multiply the length by the width. Finding the area of other shapes is not quite so easy, but there are formulas to help you.

The standard unit for measuring area is based on the size of a square. The surface of a square where all sides are one inch long is called a square inch. A short way of writing one square inch is 1 sq in or 1 in^2. A square yard is written as 1 yd^2. A square foot is written as 1 ft^2.

Tangrams

Although areas are measured in square units, the units need not be squares. This square has been divided into seven shapes, which can be arranged to make different pictures. The square and each picture have the same area, even though they look different. A square divided into seven shapes is a tangram.

Estimating areas

Estimating area is not very easy, because very different shapes can have the same area. Areas of irregular shapes can be estimated by dividing the shapes into small squares. Count the whole squares, then the bits of squares round the edges. If the bit is more than half a square, count it as a whole square. If the bit is less than half a square, do not count it.

Pythagoras was fascinated by numbers. He even founded a secret group that tried to describe the universe using numbers.

Pythagorean theorem

In the sixth century B.C. a Greek mathematician named Pythagoras proved that the area of a square drawn on the longest side of a right-angled triangle totals the areas of the squares drawn on the other two sides. The way in which he proved this has been taught for thousands of years and is called the Pythagorean theorem. The longest side of a right-angled triangle is always the one opposite the right angle. It is called the hypotenuse.

The area of the pink and green squares added together equals the area of the blue square.

Formulas for finding area

A formula uses letters to represent the length **L**, base **B**, width **W**, height **H**, or radius **R** of the shape. π is taken as about 3.14. You simply slot in the measurements in place of the letters of the formula to find the area **A**. Different shapes have different formulas. If there are two letters together, you multiply one by the other.

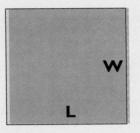

The formula for finding the area of squares and rectangles is $\mathbf{A = LW}$ (area = length × width)

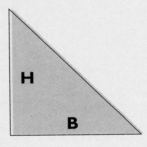

The formula for finding the area of triangles is $\mathbf{A = \frac{B \times H}{2}}$ (area = base × height ÷ 2)

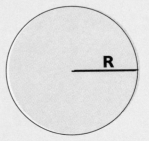

The formula for finding the area of circles is $\mathbf{A = \pi R^2}$ (area = π × radius × radius)

MEASURING VOLUMES

Measuring the volumes of cubes and cuboids is quite simple. All you have to do is multiply the length, width and height together. Finding the volumes of other shapes is not so easy, but you can use formulas to help you.

The standard unit for measuring volume is based on the size of a cube. The space taken up by a cube where all the sides measure one foot is called one cubic foot. This does not mean that one cubic foot is always cube shaped. If you were modelling with a cube of clay, you could make it any shape, but the clay would still take up the same amount of space. A short way of writing one cubic foot is $1 ft^3$. A cubic inch is written as $1 in^3$.

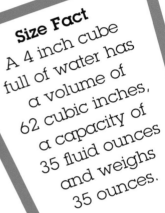

Size Fact
A 4 inch cube full of water has a volume of 62 cubic inches, a capacity of 35 fluid ounces and weighs 35 ounces.

Estimating volume

It is not so easy to estimate volume, but knowing the rough volumes of everyday things can help. For instance, a dice is about $1/2 in^3$ ($8 cm^3$). A matchbox is about $2 in^3$ ($33 cm^3$). A large suitcase is about $61,020 in^3$ ($100,000 cm^3$). One of the buildings at the John F. Kennedy Space Center in Florida has a volume of more than $4,578,000 yd^3$ ($3,500,000 m^3$). More than 3,500 family houses could fit inside.

Imagining a shape divided into cubes is not easy, but it gives the basic idea of cubic measures.

Bubble gum volume

A person once blew a bubble gum bubble that had a diameter of about 20 inches (50 centimeters). You can use the formula for finding the volume of a sphere below to find how much space the bubble took up in cubic inches. The radius of the bubble is the distance from the edge to the center, so the radius was 10 inches (25 centimeters).
It comes to a whopping 159 in³ (2616.66 cm³) which is more than the space taken up by a large beachball. The world record for a bubble gum sphere is more than 21 inches (55 centimeters) across.

Formulas for finding volume

A formula uses letters to represent the length **L**, width **W**, height **H**, or radius **R** of the shape. π is taken as 3.14.
You simply slot in the measurements in place of the letters of the formula to find the volume **V**. Different shapes have different formulas. If there are two letters together, you multiply one by the other.

cylinder

The formula for finding the volume of cylinders is $V = \pi R^2 L$
(vol = π × radius × radius × length)

cone

The formula for finding the volume of cones is $V = \dfrac{\pi R^2 H}{3}$
(vol = π × radius × radius × height ÷ 3)

cube

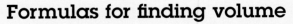

The formula for finding the volume of cubes and cuboids is $V = WHL$
(vol = width × height × length)

pyramid

The formula for finding the volume of pyramids is $V = \dfrac{WHL}{3}$
(vol = width × height × length ÷ 3)

sphere

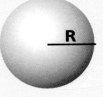

The formula for finding the volume of spheres is $V = \dfrac{4\pi R^2}{3}$
(vol = 4 × π × radius × radius ÷ 3)

A WORLD OF SIZES

Maps and globes show the different areas covered by land and sea. The real areas are scaled down so that they fit on the map or globe.

Large areas such as oceans and countries are described in units of area such as square miles. You can compare the size of things by comparing their area, volume, or perimeter.

Earth's areas

The Earth can be divided into areas of land and water. About two-thirds of the Earth's surface is covered by water. The Earth's land area is 57,688,000 square miles (148,800,000 square kilometers), while its water area is 139,000,000 square miles (361,300,000 square kilometers).

Continents

The land area is divided into continents. Each one covers many countries. Here are the seven continents and their approximate areas in square miles:

Asia	17,177,000 sq.mi.
Africa	11,697,000 sq.mi.
North America	9,357,000 sq.mi.
South America	6,868,000 sq.mi.
Antarctica	5,443,000 sq.mi.
Europe	3,843,000 sq.mi.
Oceania	3,303,000 sq.mi.

A view of the Earth from space. The vast size of the Pacific Ocean can clearly be seen. Australia, which is part of the continent of Oceania, is at the bottom left of the picture.

*This diagram shows the relative areas
of the world's seas and land masses.
The approximate areas are given below
and on page 28.*

Watery areas

The areas of the world's four oceans are:

Pacific	64,000,000 sq.mi.
Atlantic	35,657,000 sq.mi.
Indian	28,532,000 sq.mi.
Arctic	5,439,000 sq.mi.

Earth and moon volumes

The volume of the moon is approximately
21,900,000,000 cubic kilometers.
The Earth is about 50 times
larger at 1,083,208,840,000
cubic kilometers. This
means that the Earth's
volume is about the
same as 1,083,208,840,
000,000,000,000,000,000 dice.

Water volumes

Imagine a cube that measures one yard
along each side. This is one cubic yard.
Loch Ness in Scotland, home to the famous
Loch Ness monster, has a volume of about
9,840 cubic yards. It would take more than
1,500 billion buckets to empty it. This is
very small compared with the Pacific
Ocean, which has a volume of about
915,032,670,000 cubic yards.

Coastal perimeters

Africa is the continent with the most regular
coastline. This means that it has the smallest
perimeter compared to its area. Europe has
a very irregular coastline, which means it has
the largest perimeter compared to its area.

Pacific Ocean

Atlantic Ocean

Indian Ocean

Asia

Africa

North America

South America

Antarctica

Arctic Ocean

Europe

Oceania

Did you know?
The largest island is
Greenland, with an
area of 839,800
square miles.

SIZE WORDS

acre A unit of area measuring 43,560 square feet (about 4,047 square meters).

actus A Roman unit of area.

amphora A unit of liquid capacity used by the Greeks and Romans, of about 7 quarts.

area A measure that tells you how much surface something covers.

bushel A unit of dry capacity.

capacity A measure of how much something holds.

centiliter (cl) A metric unit of capacity. There are 100 centiliters in 1 liter.

circumference The perimeter, or distance, round the edge of a circle.

cord A unit used to measure wood, with a volume of 128 cubic feet.

cubic inch (in³) A metric unit of volume based on a cube where all the sides measure 1 inch.

cubic foot (ft³) A unit of volume based on a cube where all the sides measure 1 foot.

cubic yard (yd³) A unit of volume based on a cube where all the sides measure 1 yard.

deciliter (dl) A metric unit of capacity. There are 10 deciliters in 1 liter.

diameter The distance right across a circle, passing through the center.

dram (drachm) A unit of capacity. There are 8 drams in 1 fluid ounce.

dry gallon A unit of dry capacity, such as grain. There are 8 dry gallons in 1 bushel.

fluid ounce A unit of liquid capacity. In the US there are 16 fluid ounces in a pint. In Britain there are 20 fluid ounces in a pint.

gallon A unit of liquid and dry capacity.

gin A unit of capacity used by the Ancient Babylonians, equal to about 5 liters.

gur A unit of capacity used by the Ancient Babylonians.

hectare A metric unit of area based on a square where each side measures 10,000 meters.

imperial gallon A British unit of liquid capacity, equal to about 4.55 liters, or 1.202 U.S. gallons.

ka A unit of capacity used by the ancient Babylonians.

kiloliter (kl) A metric unit of capacity. There are 1000 liters in 1 kiloliter.

liter (l) A metric unit of liquid capacity, equal to the amount of water needed to fill a 10 centimeter cube.

London quarter A measure of grain. There were 8 striked bushels in a London quarter.

metretes A unit of liquid capacity used by the ancient Greeks.

milliliter (ml) A metric unit of capacity. There are 1000 milliliters in 1 liter.

minim A tiny unit of liquid. There are 480 minims in a fluid ounce.

modius A Roman unit of dry capacity.

peck A unit of dry capacity. There were 4 pecks in a bushel.

perimeter The distance all the way around the edge of a shape.

pi (π) The number obtained when you divide the circumference of a circle by its diameter. π is about 3.142.

pint A unit of dry and liquid capacity. There are 8 pints in a gallon.

quart A unit of dry and liquid capacity. There are 4 quarts in a gallon.

quartarius A Roman measure of liquid capacity.

radius The distance from the center of a circle to its edge.

sextarius A Roman unit of liquid capacity, equal to about a pint.

square *actus* A Roman unit of area equal to about 30 square yards.

square foot (ft²) A unit of area based on a square, where each side measures 1 foot.

square inch (in²) A unit of area based on a square, where each side measures 1 inch.

square mile (mi²) A unit of area based on a square, where each side measures 1 mile.

square yard (yd²) A unit of area based on a square, where each side measures 1 yd.

U.S. gallon An American unit of liquid capacity, equal to about 3.79 liters.

volume The amount of space that an object takes up.

INDEX